W9-CQE-733

Living the Boomer Life

FOR

DUMMIES®

Compliments of My Well-Being
Powered by Humana

WILEY

John Wiley & Sons, Inc.

Living the Boomer Life For Dummies®

Published by
John Wiley & Sons, Inc.
111 River St.
Hoboken, NJ 07030-5774
www.wiley.com

Publisher's Acknowledgments

Project Editor: Jennifer Tebbe

Composition Services: Indianapolis Composition Services Department

Cover Photo: ©iStockphoto.com/Nikola Miljkovic

WILEY

Table of Contents

Introduction

If you're a baby boomer approaching retirement age, you face a beautiful gift: the opportunity to fully embrace a new and exciting chapter in your life. You can start new activities, travel to the places you've always dreamed of visiting, and spend more quality time with the family and friends who mean the most to you.

Yes, approaching retirement involves some unknowns, like wondering how you'll be able to pay for all of your expenses on a fixed budget. However, by preparing yourself for those unknowns the best way you can, you'll one day be better able to do what everyone should do in their retirement years — enjoy them!

In this book, we empower you with helpful tips and expert advice on how you can get ready for retirement so you can enjoy it to the fullest.

About This Book

Living the Boomer Life For Dummies helps you get the most enjoyment out of each and every day. It's divided into four chapters; feel free to read them in order or skip around to the sections that interest you most. Either way, you'll gain the knowledge you need to prepare for and enjoy your retirement years.

Icons Used in This Book

Throughout this book, paragraphs worthy of special attention are flagged with icons. Here's what each icon means:

If you take away nothing else but the paragraphs tagged with this icon, the essentials for preparing for a happy retirement will be at the top of your mind.

This bull's-eye denotes advice that can save you time or money or just make it easier to enjoy your time to the fullest.

Watch out for this bomb and heed what you read — it'll save you from experiencing some major pitfalls!

Where to Go from Here

No need to read this book in order (although you're welcome to if that's your preference). Want to find out how to keep yourself happy as you approach or reach retirement? Head to Chapter 1. Read Chapter 2 for pointers on enjoying every moment with your loved ones and Chapter 3 for advice on leaving or remaining in the workforce. And if you're wondering how to spend all your newfound free time, flip to Chapter 4, which features information on all kinds of entertaining activities, from gardening and cooking to traveling and enjoying the great outdoors.

Chapter 1

Making Now the Best Time of Your Life

In This Chapter

▶ Discovering how staying positive helps you in the long run

▶ Using daily rituals to maintain structure in your life

▶ Mixing "want-to" with "have-to" activities for maximum enjoyment

*I*f in the past you've defined yourself by your job, you may be wondering how you could ever embrace the so-called retirement age. It may take some getting used to, but you *can* find happiness in your life without heading into an office every day or handling the many tasks that used to consume your life! This chapter helps you discover how to truly make now the best time of your life. Read on to find out why you (as a baby boomer) have the best shot at happiness, how to restructure your life so the future looks brighter than ever, and much more.

Giving Yourself the Gift of Happiness

Happiness is an important part of life — no less than anger, sadness, and fear. It begins with life itself: What mother doesn't recognize the look of happiness on the face of her newborn? Human beings are wired with an innate, neurological potential for happiness, but whether this potential eventually becomes a reality depends on how we choose to live our lives. In other words, happiness isn't a gift from the gods — it's the gift you give yourself!

Happiness is a personal state of physical, spiritual, and emotional well-being that you can experience anywhere at any time. It can be something as simple as spending a few happy moments watching your dog enjoying another day through the many different smells found around your home or yard. And as a baby boomer approaching retirement age, you're uniquely positioned to achieve this contented state.

You're in Your Prime for Feeling Sublime

Entering the 60+ (or even 50+) age group makes you part of an elite group of folks — people who have the best chance of achieving happiness with their lives. Why, you ask? Well, because age seems to increase a person's overall likelihood of being happy.

If you think that young people have the advantage here, you're wrong. Most young people are happy to be sure, but research shows that you're much *more* likely to experience happiness the older you get. Why? Because as you age:

- ✔ You're more likely to become confident about what you like and don't like in life.

- ✔ You amass a wealth of life experiences and wisdom that helps you deal with life's ups and downs.

- ✔ You develop strong relationships with friends, family, and your community that serve to support you in your endeavors.

Looking at the Benefit of Positive Emotions

Only in recent years have psychologists begun to appreciate the benefits of positive emotion — benefits that include everything from enhanced creativity to improved immune-system function (with nary a pill to be swallowed, either). The next sections reveal why positive emotions are so beneficial.

Protecting your health

You probably already know that getting upset or angry can raise your blood pressure and, in the worst-case scenario, bring on a heart attack or stroke. But did you know that positive emotions can lower your blood pressure and risk for cardiovascular disease? Well, they can, and promoting good health is another way to get the most out of your retirement!

The pioneering work of Dr. Barbara Fredrickson at the University of North Carolina illustrated that when stressed people watched a film that left them feeling amused and content, they experienced a quicker recovery of heart function. She also noted that stressed subjects who smiled while watching a sad movie had a more rapid heart-rate recovery than those who didn't smile. Her thesis is that positive emotions *undo* the effects of stress and, therefore, protect a person's health over the long run.

Other studies have shown that something as simple as getting a light touch on your hand from a compassionate friend or petting your favorite animal can also lower your blood pressure.

Broadening your focus and expanding your thinking

Positive emotions — curiosity, love, joy, contentment, wonder, excitement — expand your focus of attention. When you're angry, your focus narrows to the source of your frustration and the object of your wrath. Your mind is like a heat-seeking missile, bent on destruction.

Contrast this with what happens when you get excited about something — your mind opens up, and there's a free flow of ideas and intellectual possibility. In short, your brain works best when it's high on happiness, so let past worries or grudges go and embrace the days ahead.

Improving your ability to problem-solve

When you're frustrated and you're having trouble solving some problem that confronts you, what you need is a good laugh. Laughter unfreezes a "stuck" brain. Think of humor as a lubricant that allows the wheels — your thought processes — to once again move toward a solution. The mechanism that underlies effective problem-solving is creativity, which is your brain's ability to come up with unique answers to life's many challenges.

(So the next time you're struggling to remember something that's on the tip of your tongue, so to speak, think of a silly joke or a funny thing your dog did that morning — that forgotten item may just come to mind!)

Building physical, intellectual, and social resources

Over time, we may slow down physically and mentally and narrow our social circles to those people we have the most in common with. Making a conscious effort to demonstrate positive emotions builds the following resources and can enrich your life:

✔ **Physical resources:** People are more playful when they're happy — they're interested in golf, tennis, marathon running, pick-up basketball games, adult softball leagues, scuba-diving, and water-skiing. Happy people are also more likely to exercise on a regular basis, which helps create stronger muscles, improved heart-lung function, and increased flexibility.

The next time you feel really happy, think about signing up at a local gym. That's where all the other happy people are!

✔ **Intellectual resources:** People learn better when they're in a positive frame of mind. Think about the teachers you liked the most when you were younger. Chances are they were the ones who found ways to make education enjoyable — laughter makes kids pay attention, and attention is the key to learning. The same is true when you go to a continuing education experience; you want a speaker who is not only knowledgeable about his or her subject matter but also entertaining. By having a positive frame of mind, you'll get more out of new activities.

✔ **Social resources:** Human beings gravitate toward positive people and away from negative ones. Think about the biblical prescription, "Do onto others as you would have them do unto you," and decide how you want to be treated. If you want people to smile at you, greet them with cheer and influence their lives in some positive way. More often than not, you'll get the same in return. And since smiles don't cost a thing, why not give them away freely? The smiles you get in return will boost your spirits and help put you in a positive frame of mind.

Counteracting negative emotions

Positive and negative emotions can't exist at the same moment in time. Embracing one negates the other. For instance, happiness is one antidote to rage, and humor defuses a desire for vengeance.

The next time you're feeling upset, angry, or sad, try replacing that negative feeling with a positive one and see what happens. Think about someone who makes you laugh or something that excites you — doing so may provide just the escape you need from those negative emotions.

Living a Life of Purpose

Living a purposeful life doesn't necessarily mean that life is static. In other words, your purpose — why you're here — stays the same, but the way you spend your time can change dramatically. As a baby boomer, you're at the perfect point in your life to evaluate how you spend your time and make whatever changes you want.

Instead of searching for some task or activity that you think will give you your life's purpose, why not try to identify past experiences that made you happy and see whether you can re-create them? Here's how:

1. **Reflect on and write down the specific activity you were in the midst of and who you were with when you were the happiest you've ever been.**

   For example, writing something like "roasting marshmallows with my grandkids while telling stories" is more helpful than writing "last fall."

2. **Identify what made you so happy during that activity.**

   Was it the act of spending quality time with your grandkids? Or was it sharing part of your life with them through your stories?

3. **Think about how you can replicate that type of experience in some larger way.**

   Depending on your response in Step 2, you can invite your grandkids over for a weekend of fun and games at your house or you can offer to take them to a local history museum and share your perspective on historical events as you walk through the exhibits.

Restructuring Your Life after a Major Change

The journey of life has many twists and turns. One minute you think you know what your purpose in life is, and then everything changes. You get comfortable with one type of structure — having a career, being a parent — and suddenly you're entering a new phase of life. Then what do you do? The answer's simple: Start restructuring your life into something different yet meaningful. The following sections help you restructure your life if your children have left the home or if you're entering retirement age.

Filling the empty nest

A major life change occurs when children grow up and leave home for good. As much as you may have joked in the past about how you were looking forward to a house free of the chaos that often characterizes a home filled with kids, you may find that your empty house is eerily quiet when the kids (or grandkids) are gone. Parents who've devoted the lion's share of their time and energy to their kids suddenly find themselves with a big empty space in their lives. Some adapt easily and handle that change well; others don't and need some pointers to make this transition successfully.

If you're a parent who needs to restructure your life to get the most enjoyment out of today, follow these tips:

- ✔ **Recognize when you've accomplished your goal as a parent.** The real purpose of being a parent is to do everything you can to ensure that your child will grow into an independent adult. If you've done that, you've fulfilled that goal. Celebrate this significant accomplishment!

- ✔ **Reconnect with friends your own age whom you may have lost contact with during the years you were busy parenting.** See whether you can plug back into some activities — a golf foursome, a neighborhood bridge group — that involve having fun but don't involve kids. Or find long-lost friends on Facebook (www.facebook.com) and then seek out ways to personally interact with them in addition to staying in touch virtually.

✔ **If you're married, get reacquainted with your spouse (in other words, start dating each other again).** Take some long weekends or vacations to places you haven't been to in years but used to enjoy. Better yet, head someplace you've both always wanted to go but couldn't because of the kids.

✔ **Develop new interests that you can share with your kids when you see them.** Let them know they're not the only ones moving on in life.

Ensuring a (mentally) healthy retirement

A healthy retirement is a time of *structured freedom* — a time when you can live life on your own terms, but where you have somewhere to go and something to do each day. Without a little structure, you may find yourself watching television all day or feeling bored, unfulfilled, or even intimidated by all the free hours that retirement can offer. But with a bit of structure, each day feels like it has some purpose, and the empty spaces of free time that pepper the rest of your day feel like opportunities to look forward to filling.

If you're thinking about retiring or suspect that you may soon be asked to retire early, you need to ask yourself a lot of questions now (*before* you retire) to help you plan for the newfound availability you'll experience when you stop working. Such questions include the following:

✔ Have you considered how you'll spend your free time?

✔ Do you have any hobbies or special interests outside of work?

✔ Do you have enough projects to keep you busy?

✔ Are there things that you and your spouse like to do together — shared interests? (Chapter 2 has the scoop on the importance of shared interests in relationships.)

If your answers to these questions are more "I'm not sure" than "By all means!" then consider how you'd *like* to answer them and think about what action you can take as you prepare for retirement. If you don't have many hobbies right now because you don't have time to pursue them, think about activities you'd like to enjoy when you do have time — and then find opportunities to enjoy them! Chapter 4 presents several ideas for ways to enjoy your leisure time in retirement.

If you're already retired and are still trying to "find a fit" in this new stage of life, the advice is the same: Find somewhere to go, something meaningful to do, and someone to do it with. For instance, if you like making a difference in the lives of those less fortunate than you, why not volunteer at the local hospital? If you enjoy reading books, join a book club at your local library.

 Adding some structure by determining your interests and then finding ways to practice those passions can help you find just the right balance of having and enjoying the free time that accompanies retirement.

Using Rituals to Help You Go with the Flow

Much of everyday life is made up of *rituals* — established, predictable, patterned behaviors that structure the day. There are morning rituals (brushing your teeth, showering, reading the newspaper), midday rituals (everything from the so-called "power lunch" to a simple baloney sandwich in your office), and evening rituals (a cocktail or two, dinner at 6 p.m., a few minutes of intimate conversation with your spouse, and — if you're lucky — sex).

 Rituals are a mindless form of structure that make life flow more easily. Perhaps most importantly, rituals orient you as to where you are and what you should be doing. They're like an invisible watch — if you're taking a shower, it must be morning! Without rituals, you can find yourself wondering what happened to the day — where did all that time go?

Here are some examples of rituals you can incorporate into your life (if you haven't already):

- ✔ Exercising first thing in the morning

- ✔ Having coffee with friends at a local coffee shop

- ✔ Playing a brain game to enhance your mental health

- ✔ Getting a professional massage once a month

- ✔ Checking in via e-mail with loved ones once a day

✔ Connecting with old friends and colleagues via Facebook, LinkedIn, and other social networks

✔ Taking an afternoon nap

✔ Enjoying some quality, one-on-one time with your pet

✔ Reading for a few minutes at bedtime

✔ Spending five minutes every day reflecting on all the things you have to be grateful for

Don't become a slave to rituals — otherwise, they become tedious. If something more interesting comes along at the same time you normally take your afternoon nap, go for it! You can always nap tomorrow.

The importance of planning . . .

Lately, it seems as if human beings need a plan for everything. There are retirement planners, travel planners, wedding planners, and even people who — for a fee — will help you plan the perfect birthday party for your favorite 5-year-old.

But, as with many things in life, you *can* have too much of a good thing. Planning becomes excessive or unbalanced when every second is accounted for well in advance. No matter how many activities you're engaged in or how in-demand your time is, it's important to not over plan in order to allow room for the three Ss:

✔ **Surprise:** Everyday life seldom goes exactly according to plan. There's always a surprise or two in store for you somewhere along the way. Actually, surprises are what make one day different from the next. If your schedule is jam-packed, any surprise (even a happy one) will be seen as an intrusion and will leave you feeling stressed.

✔ **Spontaneity:** Sometimes it pays to act in the moment without a whole lot of thoughtful consideration. If a friend calls and wants you to meet her at Starbucks for coffee, don't think about whether you should or not, just say YES!

✔ **Serendipity:** The word *serendipity* literally means "happy accident." You have a moment of serendipity when you run into an old friend on the street or when an appointment is cancelled and you have an hour of unexpected free time in an otherwise busy day. You'll always have your plan. The question is, will you ever have this opportunity again?

As suggested earlier in this chapter, create some structure for the way you spend your days. While doing so, make sure to allow for the unexpected, unplanned, and unforeseen events, circumstances, and challenges that come your way each day. If you take advantage of the opportunities that fall into your lap, instead of sticking religiously to a schedule, you'll make each day one of surprise, spontaneity, and serendipity.

. . . And choosing to do absolutely nothing

Some people struggle to comprehend the psychological benefit that comes from doing absolutely nothing — that is, nothing that's productive in a material or tangible sense, like building things or making money. This concept of doing nothing can be hard to get used to after years of keeping a well-oiled household running like clockwork or producing goods, demonstrating high-level productivity, and fitting nine hours of work into an eight-hour workday. On the other hand, when you do nothing, you *produce* a state of relaxation. Funny how that works!

Here are some tips on how to spend more time doing nothing and enjoying the relaxation-producing effects of this new state of being:

- ✔ Rent a dozen of your favorite movies and spend the entire weekend watching them.

- ✔ Get up on Saturday morning and head out for the day without any agenda or destination. If something along the road to nowhere catches your eye, check it out.

- ✔ When you have an unexpected snow day and can't go anywhere, don't get dressed and don't do any chores. Think of the day as a gift!

- ✔ Spend the whole day reading your favorite novel — lose yourself in the author's world.

- ✔ Purposely lose your watch. It's much easier to do nothing if you don't know what time it is!

If you're planning on doing absolutely nothing each and every day of your retirement, that may not feel very fulfilling. Refer to the earlier "Ensuring a (mentally) healthy retirement" section for pointers on converting some of that uninspiring *nothing* into a very enjoyable *something*.

Encouraging Positivity Daily

Some of your daily experiences are no doubt significant (making your grandchild smile), while others are less so (holding the door open for someone at the store). But they're all part of what can make every one of your days positive. The next sections highlight the have-to's that fill daily life (and generate satisfaction for having accomplished them) and the want to's that bring an enhanced level of satisfaction. To get the most out of every day, seek to achieve a good mix of both.

Have-to's that generate satisfaction

You have to do this; you have to do that. You have to go here; you have to go there. You have to see him; you have to see her. These are the have-to's — things you consider essential to your social and economic survival. Most likely, they include some combination of the following:

- ✔ Going to the grocery store
- ✔ Straightening up the house
- ✔ Paying bills
- ✔ Getting the car serviced
- ✔ Visiting a friend or family member in the hospital
- ✔ Getting your flu shot
- ✔ Driving your child or grandchild to and from school
- ✔ Mowing the lawn

The more things you check off the list, the better you feel at the end of the day. You've met the basic necessities of everyday life. You're surviving, but are you *thriving?* Not unless your day also includes some things you do simply because you want to do them.

Look over the list of have-to's and check those that are on your to-do list today — and add any others that you have to do but that aren't listed here. Getting stuff done makes everyone feel good at the end of the day, even if that *stuff* is errands and small chores. To feel even better about your everyday life, build in some of the want-to's noted in the following section.

Want-to's that add sweetness to satisfaction

Think of want-to's as your hidden agenda. You want to do that, you want to go there, you want to see him or her. Want-to's are basically the icing on the cake: You can live life without them, but they sure make life a lot sweeter! Consider the following examples of classic want-to's:

- ✔ Taking a leisurely walk in the park
- ✔ Meeting a friend for lunch
- ✔ Watching a video from a funny comedian
- ✔ Reading the comics
- ✔ Browsing the racks at a new clothing store
- ✔ Checking out a blog for people over the age of 50
- ✔ Chatting with your next-door neighbor at the mailbox
- ✔ Taking a catnap

These activities are the little things that spice up your day. Use them to fill in the cracks between your have-to's — for example, meet a friend for lunch in between picking up the dry cleaning and having your tires rotated.

How many want-to's did you do today? If you're like most people, chances are you had fewer want-to experiences than have-to experiences. If your life is full of have-to's and short on want-to's, restructure your day to include a better balance of choices from both lists and watch your satisfaction with life's daily activities rise!

Chapter 2

Having Happiness at Home

*A*s a baby boomer approaching retirement age, you may be spending more time with your family than you have in the past. And by *family,* we mean the loved ones that you consider the most important people in your life — your family of birth (those you're related to) or your family of choice (friends who you'd call in the middle of the night with a worry or who you can't imagine celebrating a milestone without). Your family may be made up of either of these groups or even both (lucky you!). However your family's made up, maintaining a strong, loving relationship with your spouse, adult children, and other loved ones you see on a fairly regular basis is essential not only to your well-being but also to theirs.

In this chapter, you discover how to make the most of relationships with loved ones through prioritizing, sharing meals, and more. You also find out how to maintain meaningful relationships with those closest to you.

Setting Priorities

Some families have priorities — things they feel are most crucial to family life and success and that give the family a clearly defined sense of direction and purpose. Other families don't — they're like tumbleweeds, blowing this way and that and getting nowhere in particular.

Priorities are an important component to family success — regardless of whether your family is made up of blood relatives or close friends. They provide everyone in your family group with a sense of

- **Immediacy:** What the family needs or wants to do first and foremost
- **Purpose:** How this family wants to define itself
- **Importance:** What the family believes is important
- **Shared values:** Values that all the family members share in common
- **The future:** Where the family's heading in the days, weeks, months, and years to come
- **Stability:** An agenda that doesn't change from one day to the next

If your family could stand a little bolstering in the priorities department (and what family couldn't?), try this priority-setting exercise:

1. **Find a time when the whole family can sit down together for at least an hour.**

   If your family lives with you or lives nearby, you may be able to schedule this gathering on a weekend afternoon. If your family is spread out, then find a time of year when you'll all be together (like the holidays or a birthday celebration that everyone's able to attend). Or get an assist from technology — for a small monthly fee, you can use Skype (www.skype.com) to have a video conference with up to ten locations.

2. **Make sure everyone has a sheet of paper and ask each person to write down three priorities he or she thinks the family has or should have.**

3. **Have each person do a "show and tell," sharing his list and explaining why he chose the things he did.**

4. **Wait until everyone has shared a list and then open the door for discussion.**

After everyone has shared their priorities, evaluate them: Are there any points of agreement — things listed by more than one family member? If so, decide whether these should be some of your family's highest priorities. Are there any glaring omissions that seem like they should be addressed? If so, identify them and get input from the others. If obstacles arise during the discussion, guide the conversation to identify ways to overcome those obstacles.

Note: This exercise is also a good way to establish boundaries and responsibilities for all sorts of situations, whether you have adult children moving back home, grandkids who are going to stay with you for a while, or a loved one who needs a significant amount of your time or care.

Talking out each person's priorities gives everyone in your family group a chance to identify, examine, and strengthen the list that you all ultimately come up with. In doing so, you create an opportunity to grow and solidify the bond that you have as a family.

Balancing Interdependence with Autonomy

Striking the right balance between _autonomy_ (when offspring can live on their own) and _interdependence_ (when they can live with other people) is essential to family happiness. Children begin to strive for autonomy at the end of the first year of life, when they begin to walk. Their development of language makes them even more autonomous because they can tell their parents "No!" Autonomy really comes into its own when children enter their adolescent years. As a parent or grandparent, you need to foster this emerging sense of independence — but not at the expense of family involvement.

Interdependence means two or more people are working together on a common activity or toward a common goal. It's the old idea that two hands (or minds) are better than one. Examples of interdependent behavior among family members include helping one another prepare meals and doing household chores together.

The following sections show you how to foster autonomy without getting into power struggles with your kids or grandkids. They also explain why it's important for each family member to have a clear job description.

Sharing power

The concept of power is fundamental to family life. People talk about ways in which parents can *empower* their children, about *power struggles* between parents and children (including adult children), and the *power differential* that exists between siblings of different ages. How families handle the "power relationships" that emerge — and change — over time in large part determines how happy they end up being.

Where there's a significant imbalance of power, problems inevitably exist. Consider the case of the autocratic father who sets all the rules for his teenage daughter and expects full compliance, or the adult kids who assume their retired parents will be available for childcare or errand-running and frequently make their own plans, naively assuming these expectations will be met. At the very least, in these examples, the daughter or retired parents feel *powerless,* which can be a breeding ground for feelings of depression, defiance, or hostility. At the worst, the family members can become estranged from one another.

For parents or grandparents, the trick is to find age-appropriate ways of beginning to share power with kids, starting at an early age and continuing through adulthood. This task isn't an easy one because parents are often reluctant to relinquish power and children generally want more power than they can handle at each stage of their development. This conflict is precisely what makes family life sometimes seem more like a wrestling match than anything else.

Have a family discussion — with the *whole* family — about power. Don't allow power issues to play themselves out in an unconscious, unspoken, uncivil, and ultimately unhappy way. Ways of sharing family power at different ages include telling your 7-year-old stepdaughter that she can invite any friend she wants to the house to play, letting your 11-year-old grandson pick out which kind of pizza the family will eat, allowing adolescents of driving age to chauffeur the younger children and older members of the family to their various activities, and picking specific days of the month when retired parents can be available for childcare or errand-running.

Making sure everyone has a job

In happy families, everyone has an assignment, a job, a purpose. There are no spectators, and no one is allowed to sit idly on the sidelines.

Children — even very young ones — need to know what's expected of them. For example, you may tell your 4-year-old grandson, "Your job is to pick up your toys after you're done playing with them. That's not Grandma's job." Adolescents need to know that their job is to spend a certain amount of time helping out at home, whether their own or that of other loved ones, even though a million exciting and enticing opportunities exist elsewhere. The same goes for parents and live-in grandparents, whose jobs go way beyond simply putting food on the table and chauffeuring kids or grandkids around town.

Change the family dialogue to include the phrases "It's my job to . . ." and "It's your job to. . . ." If someone isn't happy because he doesn't like his particular job (for example, cleaning up the kitchen after dinner), tell him it's fine with you if he swaps with another family member (maybe his step-sister hates having to walk the family dog). Just make sure everyone ends up with a job so that everyone is contributing to the family's well-being.

The Family Table: Bonding Over a Regularly Shared Meal

The modern-day family finds itself with too much to do and not nearly enough time to get it all done. You're lucky if you have one meal a day together — but actually psychologists say that may be enough.

Making time to regularly enjoy a meal with family isn't about the food as much as it is about the chance to maintain those meaningful social ties that are essential to a happy family life. Among other things, mealtime is when family members can catch each other up on what's going on in their lives, ask for advice, and air their feelings without being judged.

In today's superbusy world, getting together routinely for a particular meal, such as dinner at home, may be difficult. That's fine. Have breakfast together or meet for dinner at a restaurant instead. Spending some meaningful time together each and every day is what's important.

If your family doesn't all live together, or if your family includes friends or co-workers, then try to share a weekly or monthly meal — whatever works for your particular situation. For example, gather every weekend to cheer on your favorite sports teams and enjoy Grandpa's famous grilled burgers, or host your close-knit circle of friends for lunch the third Tuesday of every month. If you live alone, aim to socialize with friends over a meal at least once a week — for example, start a dinner group where you rotate hosts and everyone contributes something to the meal (even a few dollars toward the entrée cost or an armful of fresh-picked flowers for the table can count).

Ultimately, a regularly shared meal is a time when family members of all kinds can support one another and be reminded that they belong to something greater than themselves. The location or time of day doesn't matter, but the kinship does.

Balancing the Me with the We

A balanced relationship is one where the two people involved each retain their own separate, individual identities while working together to meet life's many challenges and accomplish relationship-sustaining goals. Then again, it's naive to imagine that you can be in a happy relationship with someone — whether a romantic partner, a family member, or a close friend — without adjusting your interests, needs, and lifestyle to those of that loved one.

The hard part is deciding just how much of an adjustment to make — and that's where the idea of balance becomes important. Think about how you spend your time together — who you're with, the kinds of activities you engage in, where you go, and so on. Now decide which of these are *we* activities (the ones you both enjoy and that nurture your mutual relationship) and which are *me* pursuits (the ones that are essential for you to do for yourself to ensure your individual needs are still being met).

Examples of *we* activities include the following:

✔ Meeting others for dinner

✔ Going to a movie together

✔ Attending church together

✔ Working in the yard or going for a bike ride with one another

Me activities include the following:

✔ Playing basketball with your buddies

✔ Going to the spa with your girlfriends

✔ Having a one-on-one lunch with a close friend

How balanced are the activities you pursue for *we* and for *me?* If the numbers are too unbalanced (more than 80 percent for one type of activity and less than 20 percent for the other), it's time for a change to get closer to 50/50 — where both parties spend enough time on activities done together to maintain and strengthen the bond of partnership or friendship while still having enough time to nurture individual interests.

The key to happiness and success in any relationship lies in balance.

Three Essentials for a Successful, Healthy Relationship

Psychologists who study the recipe for a successful, loving relationship have narrowed it down to three ingredients: shared interests, intimacy, and (for romantic relationships) passion. As a baby boomer, you may find that your nest is empty and that you have more time to spend with and dedicate to loved ones. And you may identify that some of these relationships could use a little tune-up. If so, check out the following sections, which delve into the details of these essential relationship components.

Shared interests

The best thing about having a loved one who shares your interests is that you have a built-in playmate, someone to enjoy life with.

 If you feel like your interests overwhelmingly don't match those of a loved one with whom you're trying to get closer, try cultivating an interest in one thing that your loved one enjoys. Ask her what she likes about that activity and whether that's something she thinks you could grow to like. Find out all you can about the activity — the more you know, the more it may appeal to you. Or, find a new activity that neither you nor your loved one have been involved in before but that interests you both. The important thing here is not the activity itself but the fact that it's an opportunity for the two of you to do something enjoyable together.

Intimacy

When most people see the word *intimacy,* they immediately think of sex. But the kind of intimacy that leads to happiness in a relationship isn't necessarily physical and therefore applies to platonic, loving relationships as well as romantic ones. It means

- ✔ Having a closeness not found in other relationships
- ✔ Knowing the other person's secret wishes, desires, fears, and vulnerabilities
- ✔ Being cozy, warm, friendly, and comfortable
- ✔ Sharing confidences about what matters most in life
- ✔ Letting your guard down and trusting that your loved one won't take advantage of you

 If a relationship you value is short on intimacy, make a point of frequently having some time alone with each other (for romantic relationships, every day). For example, take a 30-minute walk together, meet a few times per week for coffee in the mornings, or talk on the phone most days. In these interactions, open up to your loved one and create an engaging, loving environment that encourages him or her to do the same. For romantic relationships, in addition to the aforementioned suggestions, spend

10 minutes cozying up to one another after you wake up in the morning and before you begin another busy day. Just holding each other quietly for a few minutes can speak volumes about how you feel toward each other.

Passion

In romantic relationships, *passion* is an important third component to a happy relationship. It's the feeling of arousal you get when your partner walks into the room and catches your eye. Your heart begins to pump faster, your blood pressure goes up, and everything about you gets turned on from head to toe. Passion is also the sexual interaction that comes from such feelings — having sex, certainly, but also holding hands, hugging, and touching.

Seek to have and encourage passion in your relationship by making time for physical interaction of all kinds. Hold hands on your after-dinner walk, offer a back rub after a long day, embrace one another often and for a full minute or more. Passion is all about biology and adrenaline — and the excitement of what your physical interaction may lead to!

Making Empathy the Norm

Empathy — the ability to share in another's emotions, thoughts, or feelings (in other words, to "walk in another person's shoes") — is the key to a happy relationship with any loved one. An empathetic relationship is one in which each person makes every effort to know what's going on in the mind and heart of the other. Empathy makes feelings of acceptance, appreciation, forgiveness, patience, and understanding possible. Empathy sometimes means giving your loved one a second chance, and it can open the door for alternative explanations as to why people in relationships behave the way they do.

Nearly all people have moments of empathy here and there, but often empathy is more the exception than the norm. Yet within happy relationships, empathy *is* the norm. It's consistent, predictable, and expected.

The next sections fill you in on the two main types of empathy and reveal how you can ensure they're a part of your relationships.

Emotional empathy

President Bill Clinton scored some major political points when he spoke the now-famous words: "I feel your pain." Human beings love that type of *emotional empathy* — having someone able to relate to how they feel. It's a form of emotional validation.

If you want to score some major points with your loved ones, listen to what they say and offer validation to show that you heard their concerns. Many of us are quick to suggest solutions to problems that others voice, and a lot of the time, our loved ones simply want their concerns to be heard. If a loved one says, "I'm tired," hear his or her voice. Instead of defending yourself against your loved one's feelings by saying something like, "It's not *my* fault you're tired" or, "What am I supposed to do about it?" say something like, "Of course, you're tired. Of course, you're upset. Of course, you're anxious." And mean what you say.

Rational empathy

Rational empathy is a real, authentic desire to view the world through another person's eyes. It doesn't mean that you necessarily adopt someone's way of seeing things — it just means that you try to understand and consider his or her point of view. Rational empathy, in effect, keeps married couples, families, and close friends from ending up as strangers speaking a foreign language.

To master the art of rational empathy, do the following:

- ✔ Be open-minded.
- ✔ Be considerate when sharing your beliefs and ideas.
- ✔ Be an active listener.
- ✔ Be willing to take turns in a discussion, no matter how heated it gets.

✔ Let the other person finish his or her thoughts and sentences, without interrupting.

✔ Be courteous, civil, and undemanding at all times.

✔ Be accepting of the fact that there's more than one way to see things.

✔ Be respectful of the other person.

✔ Avoid showing contempt for the other person's point of view.

The more you and your loved ones share with each other and the more you know about each another — beyond just the superficial things in life — the easier and more natural it is to "walk in their shoes."

Tending and Befriending: Reaching Out to Those You Love

Tending and befriending — reaching out to people you love — comes easy for most women. It's their nature. And it goes a long way toward easing marital tensions and making for secure and happy relationships of all kinds. But men can learn to tend and befriend. And so can women for whom tending and befriending doesn't come naturally.

Tending and befriending others involves five main elements of social behavior:

✔ **Being sympathetic or empathetic:** For example, you can say, "I know you're scared. So am I. But we'll get through this."

✔ **Being unafraid to reach out and make physical contact:** Giving your loved one a hug, patting her on the back, and holding her hand all signal to your loved one that you're in her corner and she's not alone.

✔ **Asking a loved one, "Are you okay?":** This one question helps your loved one begin to feel better and opens the door for him to share what's in his heart.

✔ **Being optimistic:** When people feel helpless and hopeless, that's when they really need someone to tell them that better times are ahead. Be that someone for the ones you love.

✔ **Focusing on the other person's needs, not your own:** Make whatever you say and do focus on your loved one. For example, don't start out by saying, "Your getting upset only upsets *me*. It only makes *me* feel guilty, like I haven't done something I should have." Instead, offer validation and a ready ear.

Remembering the Three Most Important Words

Perhaps you were expecting to find that the three most important words in any relationship are "I love you." Those words are valuable, but even more important are the words "I am sorry."

Those three words can do more for a relationship than any others. Whether it's "I'm sorry I was so selfish," "I'm sorry I hurt your feelings," "I'm sorry I forgot about our anniversary," or "I'm sorry I didn't take out the trash," saying you're sorry communicates to your loved ones that you accept responsibility for your part of the relationship and that you take ownership for any transgressions you bring to it.

And that last point is really the basis of all mature relationships — accepting responsibility for your own actions. Even the most childish and irresponsible people in the world can say "I love you" and mean it. But it takes a real adult to say "I'm sorry."

Chapter 3

Leaving the Rat Race (Or Rejoining It)

In This Chapter
▶ Looking at the budgetary realities of reaching retirement age
▶ Discovering part-time job opportunities
▶ Adjusting your current work schedule
▶ Getting into business for yourself

*J*ust because you're approaching retirement age doesn't mean you have to stop working. If you're a baby boomer who wants to work 20 hours a week rather than 40 or open that coffee shop you've always dreamed of, now's the time! This chapter offers resources on finding part-time employment and starting a business. It also provides guidance on budgeting for retirement (so that you don't have to go back to work if you don't want to) and easing into retirement by modifying your current work schedule.

Relishing Retirement or Going Back to Work

As you near retirement age, maybe you're starting to wonder whether it makes more sense for you to dive into retirement or stay in the workforce a little while longer. That's a tough decision, and only you know what call is right for your particular situation.

Following are some of the reasons why baby boomers wind up needing (or wanting) to go back to work:

- ✔ **A lack of savings:** Some retirees re-enter (or stay in) the workforce simply because they don't save up enough money to accommodate their lifestyle. Going back to work on at least a part-time basis can help supplement retirement income and provide funds for entertainment and travel. It can also help supply the cash needed for day-to-day basics (considering healthcare and other costs of living continue to rise during retirement).

- ✔ **The need to pay for medications:** Although Medicare prescription drug coverage helps retirees afford their medications to some extent, the Medicare Part D *donut hole,* where seniors suddenly find they have no drug coverage for a while, can create financial crises for many people who are dependent on a fixed income and can't afford monthly financial surprises. Continuing to work provides funds for these medical essentials.

- ✔ **The loss of a pension:** People who worked for companies for years may have been expecting a guaranteed pension only to find that, due to a company sale or bankruptcy, they're earning only about half of what they expected under the company's current employer-retirement plan. Suddenly these retirees find they have no choice but to go back to work in order to pay the bills.

- ✔ **A longing for camaraderie:** Some retirees find they miss the professional camaraderie they enjoyed in the workplace and want to return there in order to reconnect with their professional network or simply to have an additional social outlet.

- ✔ **A desire to run a business:** Eventually, some baby boomers feel they've had enough of working for others and want to start their own enterprises. Retiring from one job therefore makes it possible for them to start their dream business.

Facing the Financial Facts

Your dream retirement may include traveling to all the spots you never had time to visit, spending time with friends and family, or working on your favorite hobby. Whatever your dream as you approach or enter retirement, take the time now to make sure you'll have the funds necessary to turn that dream into a reality after you stop receiving a regular paycheck. The following sections show you how by introducing you to the four phases of retirement and the things you should budget for.

Budgeting for specific phases of retirement

When planning your budget and income needs during retirement, you need to consider several different budgets depending on the phase of retirement you're in. *Note:* You may think that you can supplement any needed funds by working, but at some point you may not be able to work, so you need to plan for that contingency as well.

Most people actually need to think of retirement in at least three different phases. And if you're planning on retiring before you can collect Social Security, then you need to think about budgets for four distinct phases. Here they are:

- ✔ **You retire before you can collect Social Security (Phase 1).** For this phase, you need to calculate financial needs without Social Security benefits and figure out how to get and pay for healthcare until you can qualify for Medicare. In many cases, you need even more cash than you did while working in order to pay for your health insurance and medical care.

- ✔ **You're retired, collecting Social Security, eligible for Medicare, and very active (Phase 2).** In this phase, in addition to Social Security, you may also be getting funds from an employer pension or drawing down funds from a retirement portfolio. Your financial needs will be a bit less than when you were working because you don't need to spend as much money (although you'll still spend some) on clothes and travel. Usually you can plan for a budget that's about 90 percent of the budget you had while working.

- ✔ **You're retired, collecting Social Security, and getting medical coverage through Medicare, but you aren't very active (Phase 3).** In this phase, you don't spend money on travel and entertainment and can usually live on about 70 percent of the income you earned while working.

- ✔ **You're collecting Social Security, benefiting from Medicare, and receiving funds from a pension or retirement plan, but your medical costs are rising as you age (Phase 4).** After you've reached this phase, you probably need about 85 percent of the income you needed while working to cover your daily needs as well as your increased medical expenses.

For additional help determining your budgetary needs in retirement, check out Social Security's Retirement Planner tool (available at www.ssa.gov/retire2). It can help you figure out how much money you'll receive from Social Security based on the most recent laws.

Knowing what to budget for

All phases of retirement require you to guesstimate a budget. Yep, your budget will be a *guess* (an educated one, but a guess nonetheless). No one can be absolutely positive of what will be needed and what the future costs will be. But, you can pretty closely gauge your costs by considering the following categories carefully when budgeting:

- ✔ **Travel and entertainment:** These activities end up on the list of most boomers' dream retirement plan. Whether you'll be able to take your desired trips or participate in your selected entertainment activities depends on how much cash you have each month. Working at least part-time helps many boomers pay for the travel and entertainment they want as part of their retirement; you may consider this solution, too.

- ✔ **Home maintenance:** If you're a homeowner, you'll need to continue paying for insurance, property taxes, maintenance, and utilities. These costs tend to rise each year, so when you're on a fixed retirement income, they can put a greater and greater strain on you financially.

Many states do give seniors a reduction in property taxes, so be sure to check with your property tax collector regarding tax benefits for seniors.

- ✔ **Food:** How much money you'll need for the food portion of your budget depends on how you plan to enjoy your meals. Many retirees go out to eat regularly with friends; others make their meals as cheaply as possible at home. Those who do have expensive dining habits are more likely to work part-time to make a little extra money to pay for their dining-out fun.

- ✔ **Healthcare:** After you're eligible for Medicare, your healthcare costs will drop, but if you retire before becoming Medicare-eligible, those few years may be very expensive.

Even if you're on Medicare, out-of-pocket costs can still be high because Medicare doesn't pay all of your expenses. Be sure to budget for healthcare costs. Needing to pay the ever-rising costs of healthcare drives more retirees back to work than any other expense factor.

If you've recently left your place of employment and health insurance isn't one of your retiree benefits, be sure to hold on to your COBRA benefits until you can find an individual health policy. COBRA is short for Consolidated Omnibus Budget Reconciliation Act, which protects your right to continuing health coverage after you leave a job. Although you must pay for the full costs of COBRA benefits, which can be very expensive, it's likely that an individual health policy will be more expensive than your group plan.

In retirement, your income is fixed, and you can't expect to get raises like you did while you were working. As your expenses increase, you'll need to cut back on other things in your budget, draw down more funds from your retirement savings, or go back to work to make some extra money.

Assessing Your Talents for Your Next Job

If you're leaning toward changing jobs or re-entering the work-force but aren't sure about the kind of job you'd like, why not discover your worker type? The sections that follow feature a quick quiz designed to help you determine the type of worker you are and the kind of work that might fit you best. The goal? To identify your strengths and lead you to a job that you'll truly enjoy doing.

Discovering what type of worker you are

Take a look at Table 3-1 and quickly circle the eight words or phrases that best fit your image of yourself. Don't spend a lot of time choosing. Also, don't cheat by looking at the explanations of the values, which follow the table.

Table 3-1		Worker-Type Worksheet	
Word	*Value*	*Word*	*Value*
Adventurous	E	Mechanically inclined	R
Analytical	I	Methodical	C
Assertive	E	Nature Lover	R
Athletic	R	Numerically inclined	C
Broad-minded	I	Obedient	C
Concrete	R	Observant	I
Conforming	C	Open	A
Conscientious	C	Optimistic	E
Cooperative	S	Orderly	C
Creative	A	Outgoing	S
Efficient	C	Patient	S
Empathetic	S	Precise	I
Energetic	E	Scholarly	I
Expressive	A	Scientific	I
Extroverted	E	Self-confident	E
Forgiving	S	Self-controlled	R
Friendly	S	Sensitive	S
Generous	S	Spontaneous	E
Helpful	S	Stable	R
Imaginative	A	Straightforward/frank	R
Innovative	S	Structured	C
Intellectually self-confident	I	Talkative	E
Intuitive	S	Unconventional	A
Logical	I	Well-organized	C

After you've finished circling the words or phrases, add up how many of each letter value you have:

A _____

C _____

E _____

I _____

R _____

S _____

You'll most likely have one dominant value of three or more and several of one or two. The dominant value matches your strongest worker type, but the other values also influence what you like to do. Here's what the values in Table 3-1 stand for:

- ✔ A = Artistic (also known as Creators)
- ✔ C = Conventional (also known as Organizers)
- ✔ E = Enterprising (also known as Persuaders)
- ✔ I = Investigative (also known as Thinkers)
- ✔ R = Realistic (also known as Doers)
- ✔ S = Social (also known as Helpers)

Picking the type of work that suits you best

This section explores the strengths of each worker type and what each type likes to do, including favorite hobbies. It also gives you some examples of possible job choices that fit each type to get you thinking about the sort of job you might like to do.

Artistic (Creators)

The skills in which Artistic people (Creators) excel include drawing; painting; playing a musical instrument; writing stories, poetry, or music; singing; acting; dancing; or fashion or interior designing. They also excel at dealing with ambiguous ideas. For fun, Artistic folks enjoy attending concerts; going to the theater; visiting art exhibits; reading fiction, plays, or poetry; working on crafts; taking photos; and expressing themselves in other creative ways.

If your worker type is Artistic, you may be able to turn your hobbies into your own business for profit. Hobbies that can successfully be turned into small businesses include photography, writing, desktop publishing, sewing, homemade crafts, painting, designing sets for plays, and speaking a foreign language.

With these skills, you may be able to find paying jobs as a copywriter, drama or English teacher, graphic or interior designer, writer, photographer, or editor.

Conventional (Organizers)

Conventional worker types (Organizers) work well within a system and can do a lot of paperwork in a short time. If you're a Conventional worker type, you also probably excel at keeping accurate records, using a computer, and writing effective business letters. You prefer and enjoy following clearly defined processes, using data-processing equipment, working with numbers, and keeping track of details.

Your hobbies may include collecting memorabilia, playing computer or card games, keeping club or family records and files, reading home magazines, and writing your family history. None of these translate easily into a small business, but your organizational skills can certainly be used to start one that assists other small businesses with record keeping, bookkeeping, or other organizational needs.

With these skills (and possibly a few courses in accounting) you could get work as an accountant or bookkeeper. You may also enjoy working as a cashier, librarian, bank teller, clerk, or data-processer.

Enterprising (Persuaders)

Enterprising worker types (Persuaders) like to initiate projects and convince others to do things their way. If this is your worker type, you likely enjoy selling things or promoting ideas, giving speeches or leading a group, and organizing activities amongst your friends and persuading others to join you.

You would likely enjoy starting your own business or campaigning for someone else in a political campaign. Your hobbies may include discussing politics, reading business journals, watching the stock market, attending meetings and conferences, and leading community organizations.

You may want to consider looking for work as a financial planner, interpreter, manufacturer's representative, salesperson, bartender, public relations representative, real estate agent, or travel agent.

Investigative (Thinkers)

Investigative worker types (Thinkers) excel at thinking abstractly, solving mathematical problems, or understanding scientific theories. If this is your worker type, you probably enjoy doing complex calculations, using a microscope or computer, and interpreting formulas. You like to work independently, using computers or working in a lab doing experiments.

You probably enjoy reading scientific or technical journals, analyzing data, and doing research to challenge your intellect. Your hobbies may include participating in a book club, studying astronomy, doing crossword puzzles, and collecting things (such as rocks, stamps, or coins). You may also like getting involved in conservation efforts or working to save an endangered species.

With these skills, the types of work you may want to consider include technical writer, science teacher, management consultant, medical lab technologist, or research analyst.

Realistic (Doers)

Realistic worker types (Doers) like to fix things, work with their hands, and be outdoors. If this is your worker type, you probably enjoy solving electrical problems, reading a blueprint, or operating tools and machinery. For fun, you may like to go camping and pitch a tent, or you may enjoy playing sports or planting a garden.

Hobbies for Realistic worker types can include refinishing furniture, growing plants and flowers, hunting and fishing, playing sports, woodworking, coaching team sports, building models, repairing cars or other equipment, target shooting, and landscaping. Most of these hobbies are good ways to make a little extra money doing things for others who aren't as good with their hands.

You may want to take a job or start your own business as an automobile mechanic, groundskeeper, painter, carpenter, electrician, or plumber.

Social (Helpers)

Social worker types (Helpers) enjoy teaching or training others. If you're a Social worker type, you can probably express yourself clearly and break down concepts into smaller pieces to make it easier for other people to learn. You usually enjoy leading a group discussion and possibly even mediating a dispute. You work well with others and enjoy planning or supervising activities, participating in meetings, and doing volunteer work.

Your hobbies likely include volunteering in social action groups, joining community organizations, and helping others with personal concerns. You also enjoy caring for children, meeting new friends, going to parties, and playing team sports or attending sporting events. You're also likely to be active in a religious organization.

You may want to consider jobs as a teacher, retirement counselor, school counselor, librarian, real estate appraiser, social worker, or mediator.

Finding a Great Part-Time Job

If you're interested in working part-time, either to make some extra cash or to have something different and fun to do, you may be wondering how to track down part-time opportunities in your area. Look no further than these fantastic resources:

✔ **Experience Works:** The nation's largest senior placement and training service, Experience Works (www.experienceworks.org), helps seniors get the training they need to find good jobs in their communities. Experience Works' largest program is the Senior Community Service Employment Program (SCSEP). Thousands of low-income people age 55 and older have been helped under SCSEP throughout the United States. To qualify for SCSEP, you must

  • Be at least 55 years old

  • Reside in a state where the SCSEP program operates

  • Have an annual family income that's no more than 125 percent of the established federal poverty income guidelines

  • Be eligible to work in the United States

  • Be unemployed

  To find out whether there's a SCSEP program near you, contact Experience Works at 866-397-9757 or 703-522-7272.

✔ **Online resources:** You can find lots of good information on the Web to help you locate companies that hire older workers. Here are some good places to start:

- Jobs4.0 (`www.jobs4point0.com`) lists job opportunities for people age 40 and older.

- PrimeCB (`www.primecb.com`) is a branch of CareerBuilder.com, the United States' largest job site. It allows you to search for jobs based on your experience level.

- Retirement Jobs (`www.retirementjobs.com`) lets you type in your zip code and instantly find jobs geared toward the 50+ age group within 5 to 50 miles of your home.

- Senior Job Bank (`www.seniorjobbank.org`) is free for job searchers and offers a wide variety of jobs, from entry level to senior executive.

Modifying Your Current Job

You may not be retired yet, but that doesn't mean you want to keep going 110 miles an hour at work every day! Sometimes the best way to prepare for retirement is to modify the structure of your current job. Two ways you can make such modifications are by going from full-time to part-time and by becoming an independent contractor. The following sections explain how to do both.

Going from full-time to part-time

The traditional way to slow down on a job is to reduce your time at work by switching to a part-time position, which would be any work assignment below what your company considers full-time (usually 35 to 40 hours a week). Part-time positions can be structured as five half days per week, three full days per week, four days per week, or any other combination of days depending on what you and your boss can work out. But to switch to part-time, you need to restructure your day and get approval for the switch.

Developing a restructuring plan

You need to do your homework before talking to your boss about working part-time. Follow these steps:

1. **Develop a detailed list of everything you do.**

   This should be a much more extensive list of your daily functions than your job description. Include even the most mundane tasks in this list, such as filing, copying, or other support functions that may not be in your official job description but are part of your daily routine.

2. **Figure out what you *must* do.**

   Obviously, if you do get permission to go part-time, you can't do everything that you were doing while working full-time, unless you have a job that really doesn't require a full-time employee. So you need to look at your list of daily functions and determine what you must do, what could be passed on to a co-worker or another department, and what could be eliminated.

3. **Create a new job description.**

   When creating a new job description, be sure to include only the functions and tasks that you can handle given the work week you prefer. Keep the tasks that are most critical to your current skills and talents.

   Also be sure to list tasks that have been assigned to you because they're a priority of your boss or your company and you've been designated as the best person to do them — even if you hate doing those tasks. You want to show your boss that your company's priorities are still important to you and that you'll continue to be a team player even as a part-timer.

4. **Evaluate the leftover tasks.**

   Determine whether the leftover tasks can be eliminated because they're "busy work" or no longer needed and then be ready to make the case for their elimination. You're sure to have some tasks left on your list that still need to be done, but that's fine as long as you believe others in your department (or possibly another department) can take over those tasks.

5. **Decide whether to recommend people/groups for certain tasks based on your relationship with your boss.**

   You may think it's better to just list tasks you don't think are critical for you to do, or you may find it better to develop a plan for who should do them.

Proposing the change

Your best shot at getting approval to switch from full-time to part-time is to ask for the change when your boss is very satisfied with your work. So develop your proposal and sit on it until the timing is right. If you're scheduled for a review and you're expecting it to be a good one, then that may be the best time to bring up the discussion. Another good time is shortly after you've completed a project for which you received positive feedback.

If your boss says no, he or she may then question whether you're still willing to put in a full-time effort or may be thinking about leaving the job. Your relationship with your boss, as well as your outstanding job reviews, could be hurt. So if your proposal is rejected, make sure to assert your commitment to your full-time job so your boss can continue to confidently count on you.

Becoming an independent contractor

If you're not ready to retire from the workforce but you'd like to be more in control of your time, you may want to consider leaving your company completely and working as an independent contractor. The beauty of being an independent contractor is that you're able to set your own schedule and decide where you want to work and how you want to work — provided you're able to meet the specifications in the contract you write between you and your employer.

As an independent contractor, you should be hired on a project-by-project basis. Your duties and responsibilities should be carefully spelled out, as well as deadlines and who will be responsible for materials, supplies, and other items that you may need to complete the project. (Make sure to seek clarification in the form of an amended contract if such specifics aren't identified to your satisfaction.) If you plan to hire assistants to help you with the project or subcontract out some of the work, be sure your costs for these items are specified in the contract as well.

When you're an employee, both you and your employer contribute to pay your taxes for Social Security and Medicare. As a contractor, however, you have to pay both employer *and* employee taxes, which means you have to pay a greater percent of your income toward Social Security and Medicare taxes.

 If a company regularly uses independent contract agreements for former employees who've retired, you may find that the company will supply you with a contract. Regardless of who generates the contract, don't sign it without first having it reviewed by an attorney who's familiar with labor law.

Buying or Starting Your Own Business or Franchise

Retirement may be just the right time to get into business for yourself. But how do you get started? And how can you figure out in advance whether it makes more sense to create your own business, purchase an existing one, or get involved with a franchise? The sections that follow offer an overview of each type of business opportunity to help you determine which one (if any) is right for you.

Starting your own business

Many baby boomers dream about being their own boss and running their own business. If you're one of these dreamers, chances are your goals for starting your own business fall into one of two categories: You're building a *going concern* (a company that has the resources to continue to operate) to fully fund your retirement, or you just want to supplement a decent retirement income. Check out the following sections for an idea of what's involved for both options.

Supplementing your retirement

If you're just looking to supplement a decent retirement income, you should consider a start-up business that doesn't require a huge upfront investment. That way you won't put any of your retirement savings at risk.

Why not start your business based on a hobby you enjoy? For instance, if you enjoy painting, you can start a paint contracting business. Or perhaps you already owned a family business but have since passed that on to your kids and now want to start something smaller to promote just within your neighborhood. For example, if you owned a construction business, you could easily start up a new home inspection company.

 If your new business is going to supplement your retirement income, then you don't have to depend on that business to live. Focus on promoting your business by word of mouth rather than investing in a massive marketing campaign.

 You can get some good ideas about how to start and run a business through the U.S. Small Business Administration (SBA; `www.sba.gov`).

Funding your retirement

If you need your new business to fund your retirement, you should expect to work more than full-time and earn very little for the first few years. A sizeable rollover of your employer-based retirement savings can help fund your personal needs during this time. *Note:* If you choose this path, you may wind up running out of money during retirement if the business doesn't succeed, so tread carefully and seek help to determine whether your plans are solid.

Here are some of the best resources you can count on if you want to start a small business:

- **Free courses:** The SBA offers an extensive array of free courses for small-business owners. It covers topics such as getting started, business management, financing, marketing and advertising, business planning tools, government contracting, risk management and cyber security, e-commerce, and taxation. To access these courses, head to `www.sba.gov/training`.

- **Service Corps of Retired Executives:** SCORE (`www.score.org`) enables retired executives to offer their volunteer services to business owners. You can get help developing and funding your business plan.

- **Small Business Development Centers:** The SBA manages the Small Business Development Center (SBDC) program as a cooperative effort among the private sector; the educational community; and federal, state, and local governments. By working with one of the 63 lead SBDCs, you can get needed management and technical assistance.

Each SBDC develops services in cooperation with the local SBA district offices to ensure statewide coordination with other available resources. You can find the SBDC service location closest to you at www.sba.gov/sbdc.

✓ **Women's Business Centers:** If you're a woman who wants to start her own business, the SBA also provides a network of almost 100 educational centers designed to assist women in starting and growing small businesses. Head to www.sba.gov and search for "Women's Business Centers" to find out more about WBCs.

Buying an existing business

If you truly need an immediate cash flow from your business to pay your mortgage and other major bills, you're probably better off buying a business that's already successful. Why? Because buying a company that has already proved it can make money and provide you with a good cash flow is a much better bet if you think you're going to need almost the equivalent of your previous full-time income. By buying a business, you can also reduce the start-up costs of time, money, and energy.

Your cash flow from the business can start immediately because you'll have inventory and *receivables* (money due from customers). You can also count on an existing customer base and an easier time raising capital.

Although it's great to have all the business basics in place — cash flow, customers, and inventory — you do have to pay for it all. The initial investment when you buy an existing business is much greater than when you start a business from scratch.

Deciding what type of business to buy

Your first step is to decide what type of business you want to buy. Your best bet is to buy a business related to the field you've in worked before. Or you could consider buying a business related to your favorite hobby or some other passion. Either way, don't look at something that you don't enjoy doing or know anything about.

Finding businesses for sale

Following are a number of sources you can turn to to find businesses that are for sale:

✔ **Business professionals:** Bankers, lawyers, accountants, insurance agents, and real estate brokers are usually the first to hear that a business may be on the market.

✔ **Suppliers for your preferred industry:** These folks often know who's thinking of selling their business.

✔ **Trade associations:** Most businesses have a trade association related to their type of business. Often employees of the association know whether one of their members wants to sell.

✔ **Newspaper ads:** Check your local business newspapers for a listing of businesses for sale, but don't count on this as your primary source for finding opportunities. Very few businesses advertise that they're for sale.

✔ **Owners of businesses you're interested in:** You never know whether a person is thinking of retiring or moving and just hasn't taken action yet.

✔ **Business brokers:** These people earn commissions from business owners who want to sell their businesses and should therefore be your last resort. Brokers only make money when they successfully sell a business, so you can't depend on them for quality advice.

If you do happen to find a business through a broker, don't count on him or her to help you through the process of *due diligence,* which is when you scour the business and its financial statements to determine whether it's a good buy. Instead, hire your own accountant and attorney to look over the deal.

Assessing the value of a business

Trying to set the value of a company can be very difficult because putting a value on intangible things such as customer base and location is tough. As the new owner of an existing business, you do have a customer base from which to build your business, but remember that most small businesses are a success because of the owner — her relationship to customers, vision, management skills, and other unique talents. Because these things can be very difficult to duplicate, put into the contract that the selling owner must be involved with the business during your first year of operation and then clearly spell out the specifics of that involvement.

When you're trying to evaluate the health of the business you're thinking of buying, as well as its future potential, you should ask to see the following records (listed in alphabetical order):

- ✔ Accounting reports
- ✔ Employee benefits
- ✔ Leases and/or building ownership
- ✔ Legal problems
- ✔ Loan documents (if you expect to assume any loans)
- ✔ Patents, trademarks, copyrights, and licenses
- ✔ Profit and loss statements and balance sheets for the past five years
- ✔ Tax returns for the past five years
- ✔ Title and title insurance
- ✔ Toxic waste
- ✔ Trade secrets
- ✔ Workers' compensation and unemployment claims
- ✔ Zoning

Talk with the company's neighbors, vendors, employees, and customers. You can get a good feel for how respected the business is and how well it treats its customers this way. A business that has a good reputation with its customers and neighboring businesses will have a much better chance of success than one that doesn't have a good reputation.

Finding a franchise

When you buy a franchise, it's like buying a business in a box. You get all the basics of how to set up your business and how to sell the product — information that's based on lessons learned while the franchisor developed and ran his or her own business.

Franchises can be a great alternative to starting your own business, especially if you don't have a lot of business or management experience, but don't expect to make much money in the first few years while you build your business.

Do, however, expect to work long hours. Well-known franchises will help you attract customers, but buying a franchise is more like starting a new business than buying an existing business.

What is franchising?

When you buy a franchise, you're actually buying a business relationship between yourself and the company that distributes a product or service nationwide. You actually buy a limited license from the company for the right to sell or distribute the product or service within a given area. Two types of franchises exist:

- **Product distribution franchises** involve an agreement between you and the manufacturer. You're granted rights to sell the manufacturer's product, but you can't operate under the manufacturer's name. Car dealerships are an example of this type of franchise.

- **Business format franchises** involve an agreement where you not only get the right to sell the product or service, but you also get an entire system for running your franchise. You also get the right to operate your business under the national brand name. McDonald's is an example of this type of franchise.

The person or company who sells the rights to you is called the *franchisor,* and you become the *franchisee* when you sign on the dotted line and buy the franchise.

How do you find one?

You've probably heard of the major fast-food franchises, such as McDonald's, Wendy's, and Burger King, but you may not be aware that there are more than 200 industry categories in which you can find a franchise today.

The primary professional association within the franchise industry is the International Franchise Association, and it groups franchises in 18 main categories, including automotive, fast food, healthcare, real estate, and travel. You can find more detail about the various industries at the IFA Web site — www.franchise.org.

If you find that the franchise you're considering isn't a member of the IFA, tread very carefully.

If you know exactly which company you want to work with, go directly to its Web site for details. If you don't, then researching and finding the right franchise for you may take some time. The good news is you can reduce that amount of time spent researching by working with a business broker. Here are three franchise business brokers that can help you find the right opportunity:

- ✔ **FranChoice** (www.franchoice.com) is the broker recommended by the IFA.

- ✔ **FranNet** (www.frannet.com) is the world's largest network of franchise consultants.

- ✔ **Entrepreneur Source** (www.theesource.com) focuses on consulting and training to help you succeed in your business.

Regardless of how you find your franchise opportunity, make sure to hire an attorney who understands franchise law and can advise you throughout the process.

Chapter 4

Living and Loving Your Leisure Time

*W*hether you realize it or not, a wealth of activities can help you occupy your time as you grow older. Want to know the best part about these activities? They can be pretty economical for any boomer. So why not dive into a new pastime or two? Depending on the activity, you may wind up with some beautiful new family memories or new skills that you can expand on over the course of the next several years. This chapter highlights some popular boomer activities you may be interested in pursuing.

Gearing Up with Great Gadgets

The 21st century has barely even begun, and already tons of amazing new devices exist. Thanks to some of this technology, staying in touch with family and friends is easier for boomers than ever. Case in point: Within just a few minutes, you can record something happening at home and share that video with loved ones thousands of miles away.

The latest and greatest technology has also made it easier to get the whole family to sign on for fun and (surprisingly) fitness in the form of video games — either the traditional variety or the kind that has you moving around. The following sections offer greater insight into the devices you may want to grab in the near future.

Staying in touch

So you want to e-mail loved ones from just about anywhere and share photos of that trip you and your spouse took last month to celebrate the start of your retirement? Why not do those things while taking advantage of some of the hottest — and easiest to use — technology on the market: the iPad and the Flip.

. . . With iPad

Apple's iPad is a combination of a killer audio and video iPod, an e-book reader, a powerful Internet communications device, a superb hand-held gaming device, and a platform for more than 150,000 apps (and probably even more by the time you read this!). This impressive device has many best-of-class features, but perhaps its most unusual feature is the lack of a physical keyboard or stylus. Instead, the iPad has a 9.7-inch super-high-resolution touchscreen that you operate using your finger. It also has a built-in sensor that detects when you rotate the device from portrait to landscape mode and instantly adjusts what's on the display accordingly.

In terms of communications power, the iPad allows you to send and receive not only text e-mail messages but also rich HTML e-mail messages (the kind with fun fonts and embedded graphics). The iPad can also read several types of file attachments, including PDFs, JPEGs, and Microsoft Word and Excel files. Even better, you can use the iPad to send and receive pictures and videos.

To use the iPad as a communications device, it helps to have access to the Internet. That's where Wi-Fi and 3G come in. *Wi-Fi* is what you use to connect to a home network or your local coffee shop network. *3G* is a cellphone technology that allows an iPad to connect to the Internet via a widespread cellular network. You can buy an iPad with only Wi-Fi or one with both Wi-Fi and 3G, but getting one that's also 3G-capable will cost you an additional $130 upfront and a certain amount per month for access from your wireless provider.

. . . With Flip

Apple's iPod has enjoyed a longtime reputation as one of the world's easiest-to-use gadgets ever, but the Flip camcorders are even easier to use. Never before has shooting and making movies been so easy. Point, shoot, save, edit (or don't bother), and share. Just like that, you're making movies and distributing them to loved ones around the country or globe!

Thanks to the Flip's small size and super easy controls, carrying a Flip wherever you go and capturing videos whenever you want becomes second nature. Whether you're RVing across the United States, hosting your grandkids over spring break, or enjoying your cat's antics, taking a video is as easy as whipping out your Flip and pressing the red Record button. Don't like what you captured? No big deal; just delete it and try again.

Sharing your videos with loved ones is pretty simple. When you plug in your Flip camcorder to your computer, a program called FlipShare opens up. You just follow the instructions for sending videos or pictures, and then your recipient receives an e-mail with a link inviting him or her to click on it and view what you sent.

Having fun

Today's video game systems offers boomers and their families an additional way to interact and enjoy some fun-filled hours together. Two of the most popular systems currently available are the Wii (made by Nintendo) and the Xbox 360 (made by Microsoft).

. . . With Wii

The Wii was the first video game system to introduce a motion-control feature: the now-classic Wii Remote. (You may have read about some Wii Remotes flying through TV screens in the early days of the Wii. The lesson there? Always wear the wrist strap!) The Wii is also really easy to use, even for video game first-timers.

Hundreds of games are available for the Wii, which means it's possible for two Wii owners to have massive game libraries that don't overlap in the slightest. That said, there's one game every

Wii owner is guaranteed to have access to: *Wii Sports,* the game that comes packaged with every Wii system sold in the United States. This is the game that gets you and up to three friends bowling, playing tennis, hitting home runs, boxing, and golfing. (Note that some games are only available for two players.)

The other fun part about the Wii is having everyone who comes over create *Miis* — cartoon-like, large-eyed, round-headed virtual versions of people. You and your friends can have fun editing your Mii's body type (by adjusting its height and weight) and playing around with its facial features (everything from facial shape, eye color and shape, and eyebrow thickness/angle to nose type, lip type, and haircut and color).

. . . With Xbox 360

If you value high-quality graphics and don't mind a system that's a bit more technologically complicated, the Xbox 360 may be the perfect video game system for you. With this system, you can (of course) play games, but you can also watch DVDs; play music directly from CDs, portable MP3 players, and standard PCs; and take advantage of features that allow you to play with others online.

Note: In late 2010, Xbox unveiled its motion-control feature — Kinect. This device allows for hands-free gaming and offers lots of fun opportunities to get you and your family members off the couch and moving.

Getting Ready for Gardening

Gardening is quite the rewarding pastime for many boomers. After all, in return for your time and effort, you receive beautiful plants that brighten your yard and delicious vegetables that supplement your meals. If you think gardening is something you might want to take up, check out the next sections, which offer an overview of tending both flowers and vegetables.

Introduce your grandchildren to gardening by having them help you plants seeds or scoop dirt into a new potted plant.

Bringing in beauty with flowers

Flowers are often the first thing that comes to mind when people think of gardening and the first thing people plan to grow when they want to beautify their surroundings. However, flowers are more than merely the beautiful display they put on. If you know the different types of flowers out there, you can take full advantage of displaying them in your garden.

Annuals

The very definition of an *annual* — a plant that goes from seed to flowering to death in one season, completing its entire life cycle in short order — states that annuals are a one-time show. When it's over, it's over. (Except when it's not; if you garden in a mild climate, many annuals merely slow down for the winter but survive.)

Annuals are hard to kill. Indeed, some of them keep blooming their cheery heads off even when you neglect them. But there is one major drawback to these perky plants: You have to buy new ones every spring. If you're planting a wide area, running out to buy more annuals year in and year out can get expensive. Time may also be an issue for you — you may grow sick and tired of getting down on your hands and knees and replanting. (If you're getting to that point, consider planting perennials, which are covered in the next section.) But annuals are great if you like a fresh look each season!

You can use annuals

- ✔ To fill an entire flowerbed
- ✔ In container displays (pots, window boxes, patio planter boxes, and more)
- ✔ To fill a hanging basket
- ✔ To edge a walkway
- ✔ To "spot" color in a perennial bed
- ✔ In edging and as decoration for a vegetable or herb garden
- ✔ To cover over or at least distract from a fading spring bulb display

Luckily, taking proper care of annuals isn't rocket science. For the most part, annuals are easygoing because they're bred to be quite tough and durable. Many can withstand some neglect and still be productive. However, you should still keep your annuals watered. You may also want to give them regular doses of plant food to help their leaves, buds, and flowers grow.

Perennials

Perennials are long-lived herbaceous (non-woody) plants — flowers and herbs, mainly. How long they last depends on the plant and the conditions in your garden. But you can certainly expect to get a minimum of two years and a maximum of a decade out of the vast majority of perennials.

A typical perennial emerges in the spring, grows and often produces flowers and seeds as the seasons progress from spring to summer to fall, and then slows down or dies back in winter. But the plant doesn't actually die; it just rests. The following spring, your perennial returns in glory to repeat the cycle.

Unlike annuals, you don't have to replant perennials yearly. Once should be enough — if you choose wisely and take good care of your perennials, you ought to get many good years out of them.

Here are some of the many uses of perennials:

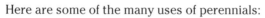

- ✔ Creating a colorful bed or border
- ✔ Filling an *island bed* (an isolated, self-contained garden, like an "island" in a sea of lawn)
- ✔ Mixing them with annuals to ensure summer-long color
- ✔ Edging a walkway, patio, pool area, or deck
- ✔ Inter-planting them with roses or other ornamental shrubs to provide year-round interest
- ✔ Dressing up an area that was formerly lawn

Nothing makes newly planted perennials feel more welcome than plentiful water. The perennials have gone from a sheltered and confining life in a pot to the wide world of your garden, and water helps sustain the roots and encourages them to establish themselves and expand into their new home.

When it comes to food, many perennials (like most people) enjoy being fed. They respond by growing more robustly and producing more flowers. You're fine with a general, all-purpose garden fertilizer; apply it according to the label directions during the height of the growing season.

Producing your own produce

When's the best time to start planning a veggie garden? Right now! When considering where to plop down your plot, look for a spot

- ✔ Close to the house that you walk by daily so you don't forget about your project
- ✔ That gets at least 6 hours of direct sun a day
- ✔ That has great soil

Don't be discouraged if you lack the ideal garden spot — few gardeners have one. Just make the most of what you have, including containers for vegetables that don't need a lot of horizontal space, like tomatoes and herbs.

The next sections highlight the kinds of vegetables you can grow and provide some pointers on starting your first veggie garden.

Surveying the veggies you can grow

What should you put in your new garden? Well, you can grow many different types of vegetables in your yard — and not just in the backyard. These days veggies are pretty enough to be front and center. Here are just some of the vegetables you can plant:

- ✔ Tomatoes
- ✔ Peppers and eggplants
- ✔ Carrots, onions, and potatoes
- ✔ Peas and beans
- ✔ Cucumbers, melons, pumpkins, and squash
- ✔ Broccoli, Brussels sprouts, cabbage, and cauliflower
- ✔ Lettuce, spinach, and Swiss chard

Choosing between seeds and transplants

The easiest way to start a new garden is to grow vegetables that can be planted from seed directly into the soil. For veggies that are best transplanted, buy the transplants locally. (Some vegetables can go both ways, too.) Here's a breakdown of the two groups:

✔ Vegetables that can be sown directly into the ground as seeds include beans, peas, carrots, beets, and sweet corn.

✔ Vegetables and herbs you can find in local garden centers as transplants include tomatoes, peppers, eggplants, broccoli, cauliflower, cabbage, lettuce, cucumber, squash, basil, and parsley.

If you have a small garden, go with the transplants. If you're growing a larger garden, you'll find it less expensive to grow veggies from seed.

Working the soil

After you have your vegetable seeds or transplants ready to go, the temptation is to simply turn the soil and then plant. However, soil building is one of the most important parts of any boomer's gardening experience. Your soil needs to be fertile, loose, dried out, and relatively weed- and rock-free to grow the best crops. If you take care of the soil in your beds, it'll take care of you by producing healthy, productive vegetables with few insect and disease problems.

Spend some time working the soil by hand or with a tiller. Amend it every year with compost to keep the fertility high and make it more workable. Also, test your soil to see whether it needs other nutrients — simply use a do-it-yourself testing kit found at a nursery (or go to www.dummies.com/how-to/content/how-to-test-your-soil.html for more specifics).

Keeping your garden growing and enjoying the rewards

When your garden is up and running, you can lower your maintenance time and effort and raise your satisfaction level by doing the following:

✔ Mulching your beds

✔ Watering your plants deeply and consistently

✔ Fertilizing when necessary

No matter how well you care for your garden, pests still may attack your plants. It's best to grow insect- and disease-resistant varieties when possible. And be sure to create barriers to block pests from attacking, clean up the garden well to remove overwintering insects and diseases, and spray only as a last resort.

Now for the fun part: harvesting. Check the garden daily when plants are producing and pick even if you don't have room in the refrigerator. With many vegetable plants, the more fruits you pick, the more you'll get. You can always give away the fresh produce to friends, family, and neighbors, so don't stop picking.

The Essentials of Cooking

If your cooking skills are limited but you've always dreamed of whipping up frittatas and fricassees, why not look into improving your cooking skills? The following sections review basic cooking techniques and meal-planning pointers. They also provide tips from chefs to get you slicing and dicing with the best of 'em!

Presenting basic cooking techniques

Recipes are often full of terminology and techniques that may be unfamiliar to you, yet at the heart of most recipes are some basic techniques. Become familiar with the terms in the following list, practice the techniques, and you'll realize that many recipes aren't as complicated as you thought.

- ✔ **Boiling, poaching, and steaming:** These terms involve cooking with water. *Boiling* is heating water so that it bubbles vigorously. *Poaching* is cooking fish, eggs, or vegetables in gently simmering water — water that's just beginning to bubble but not yet boil. *Steaming* is cooking food over, but not in, boiling or simmering water.

- ✔ **Sautéing:** This term refers to cooking food in a skillet or sauté pan quickly over high or medium-high heat, usually in heated oil or butter.

- ✔ **Braising and stewing:** To *braise* is to cook food in a small amount of liquid, such as water or broth, for a long period of time. This technique results in particularly succulent meat. *Stewing* is cooking food (usually meat and veggies) in liquid flavored with herbs, broth, and sometimes wine until it's absorbed, creating a delectable, too-thick-to-be-soup concoction.

✔ **Roasting:** *Roasting* involves cooking food, uncovered, in a pan in the oven for a long period of time. This technique is usually used to describe cooking vegetables or large pieces of meat, such as a pot roast or a turkey.

✔ **Grilling:** If you like to spend as much time as possible outdoors, *grilling*, or cooking on a grate over hot charcoal or other heat element, is for you. Grill varieties include charcoal, gas, and electric.

Stocking up on pantry staples

The payoff for keeping a well-stocked kitchen, with only enough perishables that you can eat in a week, is that you can whip up satisfying meals on short notice. Following are a series of checklists of pantry basics (be creative and think of some ways to incorporate them into your everyday meal planning!).

Bottled, canned, and dry goods:

✔ Assorted breads, buns, and English muffins

✔ Assorted oils and vinegars (think olive oil, balsamic vinegar, and red wine vinegar, to name a few)

✔ Canned and dried beans

✔ Cold and hot cereals

✔ Garlic and onions

✔ Macaroni, spaghetti, and other pasta

✔ Olives

✔ Potatoes

✔ Roasted peppers

✔ Spices (aside from salt and pepper, basil, bay leaves, chili powder, ground cumin, oregano, and parsley are often good to have on hand)

✔ Tomato paste and canned tomatoes

✔ Dried grains, such as white, brown, and wild rice

✔ Wines (a dry white and a dry red are good for adding to sauces)

Condiments:

- ✔ Dijon-style mustard
- ✔ Ketchup
- ✔ Mayonnaise
- ✔ Salad dressing
- ✔ Salsa
- ✔ Soy sauce
- ✔ Tabasco or other hot sauce
- ✔ Worcestershire sauce

Refrigerator and freezer goods:

- ✔ Cottage cheese and cream cheese
- ✔ Eggs
- ✔ Frozen chicken breasts
- ✔ Frozen tilapia filets
- ✔ Hard and semihard cheeses (such as mozzarella, Parmesan, cheddar, and blue cheese)
- ✔ Milk
- ✔ Pizza dough (either frozen or refrigerated)
- ✔ Produce (apples, bell peppers, carrots, grapes, salad greens, spinach, and tomatoes are all healthy, multipurpose options)
- ✔ Sour cream and plain yogurt
- ✔ Sweet (unsalted) butter

Planning your menu

Writing out a shopping list is likely something you've done thousands of times, and doing so ensures that you have everything you need for your meals before you start cooking. Some boomers like to write down all the elements of each meal for an entire week at a time and then study recipes and make out a shopping list. But you don't have to be quite so formal, especially when trying out new recipes or cooking techniques. Simply make sure you have all the necessary ingredients and equipment to cook all the elements of a meal before you begin.

But how do you know what to make? For most families, a simple meal with a main course (a meat or vegetarian dish, featuring ingredients separately or in casserole form) accompanied by soup or a salad and a starch (bread, potato, rice, pasta, or some other grain) make a filling and complete meal. If you want to make a more formal meal, add an appetizer, include a salad or soup and serve either (or both) before the entrée, and then serve a vegetable alongside your entrée and starch.

As you gain cooking prowess, feature a tasty new vegetable preparation several times a week (perhaps featuring some of your home-grown produce), or make your own risotto or seasoned rice versus selecting something that starts in a box. Consider serving the proteins that your family enjoys but try using different techniques to cook them — grill pork even in winter, braise chicken for a delicious stew, steam delicate fish for a healthy and tasty supper. Meals don't have to be elaborate, especially lunch: a hearty salad or a big bowl of home-made soup often hits the spot.

Thinking like a chef

The following advice is straight from the pros and applies to boomers of all skill levels. Take it to heart, and you'll find yourself progressing as a cook faster than you expected.

- ✔ **Know the basic techniques.** Cooking is so much more fun — and successful — when you approach it with confidence, and confidence arises from knowing your techniques so well that they're second nature (see the earlier "Presenting basic cooking techniques" section for help familiarizing yourself with all the basics).

- ✔ **Use only the freshest ingredients and buy only in-season fresh fruit and vegetables.** Seasonal produce offers the highest quality and supply and the lowest price. Let what's fresh and available at the market help you spontaneously decide what's for dinner.

- ✔ **Prepare ingredients before you start cooking.** Get the chopping, mincing, deboning, and washing chores out of the way in order to create an even, efficient flow of cooking steps.

✓ **Get to know herbs — both fresh and dried — so you can season without relying on a recipe.** Chefs base some of the world's great cuisines on the combination of herbs and spices.

✓ **Plan your menus in advance.** Before cooking, think about contrasting flavors, textures, and colors. Keep the courses balanced and don't overload yourself. If you serve a time-consuming, complex appetizer, serve a simple entrée or one that needs only reheating, like a tasty stew.

✓ **Be thrifty.** Throw out nothing (unless of course it's spoiled). Every morsel of food is usable for soups, stocks, salads, and so on. Plus you can often make great meals from leftovers.

✓ **Don't be a slave to recipes.** Use a good, basic recipe that you like as a starting point, but don't consider it written in stone. With experience and good technique, and by discovering how ingredients work together, you can simply glance at a recipe and make adjustments to suit your taste.

✓ **Have fun.** Take a cooking course, buy yourself a cookbook, or make a new dish that you've always wanted to try. Cooking should always be fun! (Note that an easy way to add enjoyment to cooking is to have your grandkids help with simple tasks, like stirring a sauce or frosting cupcakes.)

Getting Cultured: New York Theater and Museums

Taking in a little culture (in the form of museums and live theater) is an easy way to spend an afternoon or evening, and it's a great opportunity to expand your knowledge base of and appreciation for subjects such as history and the arts. In the United States, there's no doubt about it: New York's theater scene is second to none, and its museums are outstanding.

Arguably, nowhere else in the United States can you find such a diverse and plentiful offering of top-notch theaters and museums than the Big Apple. With such a variety, you're sure to find enjoyable, affordable attractions to satisfy anyone you travel with. Check out the next sections for details on scoring discounted show tickets, finding the don't-miss destinations, and more.

Taking in New York theater

Three different categories of New York theater exist: Broadway, Off-Broadway, and Off-Off-Broadway. These terms refer to the theater size and pay scales, not location.

Broadway gets the most ink and the most airplay. It's where you find the big stage productions, from crowd-pleasing warhorses like *The Lion King* and *Mamma Mia!* to phenomenally successful shows like *Wicked* and *Avenue Q*. Most of the Broadway theaters are in Times Square, dotting the side streets that intersect Broadway. Unlike Broadway, Off-Broadway can be anywhere. Off-Off-Broadway shows tend to be more avant-garde, experimental, and/or nomadic (and also have the cheapest ticket prices). Off- and Off-Off-Broadway productions tend to be based downtown, but mini theater districts exist in Midtown and on the Upper West Side as well.

Broadway shows typically have eight performances a week, with evening shows (which usually start at 8 p.m.) on Tuesday through Saturday. Matinees usually take place on Wednesday and Saturday at 2 p.m. and Sunday at 3 p.m. (Schedules can vary, so confirm performance times at the box office.) Broadway and Off-Broadway shows usually start exactly on time; if you arrive late, you may have to wait until after the first act to take your seat. ***Remember:*** Be on time so you don't miss any of the show!

If you hear that an actor you want to see is coming to the New York stage, don't put off your travel and ticket-buying plans. Stars' runs on stage are often limited, and tickets for their shows tend to sell out fast. The box office can tell you how long a star is contracted for a role.

Scoring discounted theater tickets

Ticket prices for Broadway shows vary dramatically. Expect to pay a lot for good seats — $100 to $150 or more for full-price tickets to any given show. The cheapest end of the price range can be around $25 to $50, depending on the theater configuration. If you're buying tickets at the low end of the available range, be aware that you may be buying obstructed-view seats. If all tickets are the same price or the range is small, you can count on all the seats being pretty good.

Off-Broadway and Off-Off-Broadway shows tend to be cheaper than Broadway shows, with tickets often as low as $10 or $15. However, seats for the most established shows and those with star power can command much higher prices, from $60 and up.

If you're planning to get to as many shows as you can while you're in New York, it's worth it to register with a service like Theatermania.com, Playbill.com, or Broadway.com to get discounts and subscribe to their e-mail newsletters.

For same-day Broadway and Off-Broadway tickets at a discount (up to 50 percent), try visiting the TKTS booths. The permanent booth is in the heart of the Theater District in Duffy Square at 47th and Broadway. For the most up-to-date ticket information, consult www.tdf.org; you can also call 212-221-0013. *Note:* Before you visit a TKTS booth, keep in mind that long lines are the norm and you're not guaranteed to get tickets for a specific show. (Also, tickets for a popular show may be available because the cast for that day changed, which isn't the best scenario if you have your heart set on seeing a particular production or actor.)

Some long-running shows have special promotions, so it pays to call the box office of the theater where the show is playing and inquire. As a last resort, remember that a cheap way to get a seat is not to have one: Standing room is available at some shows for $20 to $35.

Feeling the lure of the Big Apple's museums

If you're a museum junkie, you'll feel right at home in New York, which boasts such gems as the Museum of Modern Art, the Cloisters, Ellis Island, and the Frick Collection.

But don't just assume that the only museums worth seeing are on the island of Manhattan. Brooklyn and Queens are destinations in their own right, and the Bronx also offers worthwhile attractions. You can visit the Bronx Zoo (after all, isn't a zoo just like a museum full of animals?), the Brooklyn Museum of Art, and the Museum of the Moving Image in Queens.

To save cash while touring New York's great museums, focus on visiting those that have a "suggested donation." Or just go on the days and nights that are free.

Zeroing in on don't-miss destinations

New York offers boomers a hundred great things to see, and if you had all the time in the world, you might be able to see about half of them. But chances are you have just a few days to hit the highlights. So why not make a point of visiting these don't-miss destinations?

- **Shakespeare in Central Park:** This New York institution involves the staging of two plays each summer at the open-air Delacorte Theater in Central Park. Best of all, the performances are free. Two shows are offered (usually a Shakespeare play featuring a large company and a more modern theater classic), and the productions run from June to August. For more information about Shakespeare in the Park, contact the Public Theater at 212-539-8500 or visit www.publictheater.org.

- **American Museum of Natural History:** This vast museum, which spans four city blocks, features a remarkable permanent collection of taxidermic wildlife; an enormous exhibition dedicated to biodiversity; interactive exhibits; and displays of gems, dinosaur fossils, and meteorites, among other treasures. Visit www.amnh.org or call 212-769-5100 for more information.

- **Metropolitan Museum of Art:** From its world-famous Egyptian collection to its massive holdings of American and European masterpieces to its beautiful sculpture garden, the Met has something for everyone. Visit www.metmuseum.org or call 212-535-7710 for more information.

- **The Paley Center for Media:** With more than 140,000 radio and television programs in its permanent collection, this museum is more like a library in that you can "check out" recordings or programs and play them in audiovisual cubicles. For more information, call 212-621-6800 or visit www.paleycenter.org.

> ✔ **The Children's Museum of Manhattan:** Designed for children ages 2 to 12 (and just as enjoyable for kids at heart), this museum is strictly hands-on. Its five floors include a Dora the Explorer–themed section; PlayWorks, especially for children age 4 and under; and a reading center for quiet time. Call 212-721-1234 or visit www.cmom.org for more info.

Get Outdoors: Camping, Hiking, and Biking

Retirement age can be a perfect time to get back in touch with nature, whether that means camping with your family or friends, hiking, biking, or fishing in some ideal locale. Enjoying outdoor activities just makes you feel *good*. The fresh air is energizing and encourages you to take deep breaths, and you get good cardio and strength benefits by moving your muscles and bearing weight on your bones (even just by walking!). All that nature helps boost your spirits, too, whether you're able to gaze at a field of wildflowers while hiking or enjoy a mulched plot while walking around a local park. The sections that follow give you some pointers on enjoying these outdoor activities.

No matter which outdoor activity you engage in, staying active is essential to maintaining (or even improving) your physical health. It can also help boost your mental health thanks to the endorphins that pump through your body when you exercise and the camaraderie you feel and bonds you create when you participate in group physical activity.

Forget a roof and four walls: Enjoying camping

Camping with family or friends is an outstanding way for boomers to share a love for the outdoors without breaking the budget. It takes lots of planning and loads of patience, but it's ultimately a rewarding activity for everyone involved.

Setting up camp is really pretty simple. Just make sure you do the following:

✔ **Find a good campsite.** The perfect campsite is usually level, with a relatively rock- and root-free spot to pitch your tent. So use your eyes and look for level sites that have naturally adequate drainage and aren't sensitive areas that will be irreparably damaged by your presence.

In hot weather, an open site located on top of a hill or ridge may offer a cooling breeze — which can also help to minimize bugs. (In cool or windy weather, it's wise to avoid such sites.) Also, campsites surrounded by trees offer privacy and protection from the sun. Keep in mind that the closer you are to a stream or body of water in a valley bottom, the colder the night will be.

✔ **Pitch the tent.** In the grand scheme of campsite setup, erecting the tent should be the first order of business. Find the smoothest, most level surface for your tent site. Lay down a protective ground cloth as a barrier against moisture and rain and then spread out the tent over the top of the cloth. Face the tent in any direction you want (although a scenic view is always a good choice).

✔ **Keep your campsite clean.** Garbage, food, and dirty dishes attract animals and insects. Keeping your site neat and tidy is always worth the very small effort it takes, so leave a trash bag set up and handy for all litter to go into. And when eating in a campground, eat over a tarp and then use a whiskbroom to sweep up the crumbs and food debris so those little morsels don't attract insects.

✔ **Shut down for the night.** Securing your campsite before you bed down for the night is the best way to avoid inviting problems during the night or in the morning — not the least of which is clothing and gear that has disappeared by claw or wind. Be sure to gather water, clean the dishes, hang or store food properly, secure loose items around the camp, arrange important personal gear, lay out emergency items within easy reach of your sleeping bag, and check the tent to make sure it's secure.

Take a hike!

Hiking is a great way to get some exercise while enjoying the great outdoors. As with many outdoor pursuits, you'll have the most fun if you plan your hike before you head out and if you keep some important pointers in mind.

Deciding how long to hike

How far you're going to hike depends on a combination of things, including the purpose of the hike, the age and experience of the hikers, the type of terrain you're hiking on, and the time of day. Most people hike at a rate of 3 to 4 miles per hour on flat to rolling terrain without too many obstacles to step over and around. So if you intend to take a half-day hike, plan to cover a maximum of about 12 miles.

If the goal of your hike is to watch nature and enjoy a casual stroll, plan on a much shorter hike to ensure plenty of time for stopping and enjoying. Also consider the age and fitness level of the hikers in your group — make sure your hike isn't more ambitious than the youngest or least fit hiker can easily accommodate.

Picking your hiking path

You generally have three types of hiking trails to choose from:

- ✔ **Loop trails** are easy. You start hiking, wander around the loop, and end back where you started.

- ✔ **Out-and-back trails** take you out one way until you have to turn around and return the way you came. These trails are ideal if time is short and you want to speed your return trip.

- ✔ **One-way trails** are trails that you can hike only one way, so you need a ride when you get to the end.

Reading trail markings

As you travel across wildlands, you'll encounter a wide variety of marking trails, as noted in the following list:

- ✔ **Paint markings** are straight brush strokes or a circle and are often found on rocks or trees. Simply follow the same color paint along the route to stay on track.

- ✔ **Blazes,** mostly found in the old-growth forests of Canada and the Eastern United States, are physical cuts into a tree that leave a mark you can follow.

- ✔ **Cairns or ducks** are stacks of rocks along a rocky, tree-less route. Cairns are frequently used through boulder fields or in alpine environments where no other means for providing a sign exists.

No matter what type of trail you pick, by allowing enough time to enjoy the outing and keeping a sharp eye for the trail markers, you and your companions can look forward to hours of outdoor enjoyment.

Joining in: The joys of social bicycling

Simple math doesn't cut it in the bicycle world. If one bicycle is a good thing, then two is a lot more than twice as good! Riding is a great way to get off the couch, meet people, push your limits, and maybe even do a good deed while enjoying the great outdoors.

Partnering up

You remember when you were a kid and you'd just go over to your friend's house and say, "Hey, wanna ride bikes?" Well, although nothing else in your life seems quite that simple anymore, riding a bike can be. All you have to do is find a biking buddy — someone with a similar schedule and who can keep up with you (and vice versa). A biking buddy can be your spouse; your son, daughter, or grandchild; a neighbor; a friend; or a co-worker.

Club rides

Soon after joining a biking club, you'll find the more-the-merrier factor at work when lots of people gather together for the same reason: turning the pedals. Often the most rewarding moments of belonging to a club come when you're hanging around the parking lot before or after a ride. Anybody wearing a helmet becomes an instant acquaintance — and maybe, before long, a friend.

To find a biking club in your community, start by asking around at a local bike shop. Then check out the community calendar section of the local newspaper and start searching the Web. Most clubs welcome new members, even complete beginners. **Remember:** Make sure you're honest about your abilities when talking to the ride organizer; most clubs offer rides at different paces, and you want to make sure you're steered to a ride that's just right for you.

Charity rides

More and more charities are using bike rides as a way to raise money and consciousness. The AIDs ride, The Tour de Cure sponsored by the American Diabetes Association, the MS-150 to support multiple sclerosis research, and the American Lung Association's transcontinental Big Ride are just a few of the nation's biggest charity events, but they're far from the only ones. You can track down other charity bike rides by checking in with the usual suspects: your local bike shop/club or the Web.

Be sure to get information on charity rides well in advance. Most of these events involve a good bit of riding — anywhere from 25 to more than 100 miles in a day — so not only will you need time to collect pledges, but chances are you'll also need a little time to get in shape.

Bicycling vacations

When it comes to a two-wheeled vacation, the options for boomers are varied: The locations can range from Death Valley to the rolling hills of Vermont to the mountains of the Alps. Themes can range from gonzo mountain biking to mellow eat-and-ride gourmet getaways to literally following the path of the famed Tour de France bike race.

Cycling magazines such as *Bike* and *Bicycling,* as well as general outdoors magazines such as *Outside* and *Men's Journal,* run stories about cycling vacations, generally in the late winter and early spring. Not coincidentally, these same publications also run advertisements from companies that organize such vacations. Word of mouth also works well; ask your riding friends about cycling trips.

Top fishing destinations

If fishing, or *angling,* floats your boat, then consider spending a portion of your retirement scoping out some of the top local fishing destinations. The United States is home to several great fishing destinations, including the following:

✔ **The Freshwater Everglades, Florida:** Stretching south from Lake Okechobee to the mangrove-dotted brackish waters just north of Florida Bay, these stands of waving sawgrass are criss-crossed by bass-filled canals and offer dependable action for spunky largemouth. The Sawgrass, Holiday Park, and Loxahatchee refuges all offer angling access.

✔ **Montauk Point, New York:** Pretty much every striper, bluefish, tuna, marlin, weakfish, and shark in the northwestern Atlantic has to pass by this rocky outcropping at the tip of Long Island twice a year: once on the northern migration and once on the return southern trip in the fall.

✔ **Slough Creek, Yellowstone Park:** With no trees to obstruct your backcast and very little in the way of subsurface obstructions to wrap your line, this is a great place to land a big trout on very light tackle.

✔ **The Missouri River, Montana:** The section of the Missouri below the dam at the confluence at Three Forks is a mind-bogglingly rich spring creek full of football-sized trout gorging themselves on unending hatches of all kinds of insects.

✔ **The Meramec River, Missouri:** This lazy, meandering, limestone-enriched river is easy to float by yourself and full of great smallmouth bass on their home range.

✔ **Ellis Island, New York Harbor:** On Christmas Eve, the die-hard flyrodder can fish beneath the causeway that leads from Ellis Island to Jersey City. With the skyline of Manhattan as a backdrop and the city all decked out in Christmas lights, this is great fishing at a magic time.

Depending on the type of fishing you participate in, angling may not have as many physical benefits as other outdoor activities described in this chapter. However, the peace and quiet that often accompany fishing give your mind a chance to wind down and relax (a sometimes hard task to achieve these days). This quiet time also gives you the perfect opportunity for some reflection or an opening to share with family or friends the thoughts and feelings that may not get much of a voice during hectic, everyday lives. Whether you catch that night's dinner or end the day with a great story about "the one that got away," the rewards of fishing are plentiful.